RICHMOND AND KEW GREEN

A Souvenir Guide

by Nicholas Reed

Published by

LILBURNE PRESS
1 DOVER HOUSE
MAPLE ROAD
LONDON
SE20 8EN
TEL: 0208 659 5776

First Edition
November 1992

ISBN 0 9515258 6 7

INTRODUCTION

This book introduces visitors to the history and delights of Richmond Town and Kew Village, by means of three historical walks.

The first walk (page 2) takes you around Richmond centre and along the river. This should take about one hour.

The second (page 27) leads you up Richmond Hill and then back. This should take about 1½ hours.

The third (page 39) leads from Kew Gardens Station to Kew Green and then to Kew Church. Following the walk from the Station up to the main entrance gates of Kew Gardens should take about an hour.

GETTING TO RICHMOND

A Special Request: <u>Please use public transport!</u>

Richmond is probably the easiest place in the London metropolis to reach by public transport. It is served by District Line tube from Victoria, by train from Waterloo or Clapham Junction, from West Hampstead on the Inner London Loop, or by several buses. During the summer, Richmond can most attractively be reached by boat either downstream from Kingston or Hampton Court, or upstream from Westminster or Kew. So our heartfelt plea is: please don't use your car, and leave car travel to those who have no alternative, such as the disabled.

For such people, traffic congestion around Richmond is severe, and parking is also very difficult. But there is a large car park approached from the Twickenham Road (A316); there is also a multi-storey car park beside Richmond Station, though this is often full.

Facilities: Public conveniences are constantly being closed down either temporarily or permanently: we take no responsibility for their availability! But at the time of writing there are conveniences in Richmond Station, and beside the entrance to the Old Town Hall, which we shall pass later in this first Walk. (There are also conveniences next to Waitrose in Sheen Road.)

TWO HISTORICAL WALKS AROUND OLD RICHMOND

1) RICHMOND GREEN AND THE RIVER

Our first walk starts from Richmond Station. The railway came to Richmond in 1846, though the station building we now see dates principally from 1937. On emerging from the Station, turn left, and cross the main road at the pedestrian crossing opposite Oriel House. Once across, turn right and almost immediately left, and one finds oneself walking down a brick-lined pathway next to no 26.

We emerge on a roadway with, to the right, some fine old Georgian houses in the road called Parkshot. To their right stood a similar group, now replaced by the Magistrates Court; at no 8 Parkshot the novelist George Eliot lived during the 1850s, and wrote 'Adam Bede' while there. (Two years after her husband's death in 1880, when she was sixty, she was to shock her best friend, Mrs Georgiana Burne-Jones, the wife of the pre-Raphaelite, by marrying a man twenty years younger than herself.)

From this pathway we turn left, cross over the brick railway-bridge, and see on the right, Little Green. This was a piece of open land given by Charles II to be used as a bowling green. In 1765 it became part of George III's royal garden, and still remains royal land, as does much of the land around it. Continue further, past Richmond's Central Lending Library, to find Richmond Theatre on your left.

This is the last of the several theatres Richmond has had in the past: the first being opened on Richmond Hill in 1718. The current building was completed in 1899, and the two foundation tablets, on opposite corners of the building, commemorate Mr and Mrs Mouflet, who funded the new theatre, and Frank Matcham, who designed it. With its distinctive terracotta facade, and green onion-shaped cupolas of copper, one can see how even a striking Victorian building need not spoil the look of the rest of the Green; after all, it does not stand on the Green proper, and is attractive in its own right. The Theatre was completely renovated in 1989-91 and reopened in November 1991. Continuing up to Duke Street, one can now see the whole expanse of the larger Richmond Green.

Above: Richmond Theatre, newly renovated

Richmond Green is a microcosm of the ways in which the town saw itself during the centuries. In medieval times, being set beside the royal manor-house, jousting and tournaments were held on the Green. By the time Queen Elizabeth took up residence in what was now the Royal Palace, more common entertainments, like bull- or bear-baiting, were held here; archers practised their marksmanship, while at other times sheep were grazed on its grass. In the 18th century, prize fights (boxing without boxing gloves) were held here. Nowadays, it is best known for its cricket, which has been taking place here since at least 1666, the year of the Great Fire of London. Richmond's May Fayre also takes place on the Green on the second Saturday in May.

Nos 1-3 Richmond Green: Shakespeare House at left

On the corner of Duke Street, facing the Green, is Shakespeare House, with its splendid portico and attractive attic windows. The house itself as we now see it is thought to have been built too late to have accommodated Shakespeare, though parts of the interior may go back to his time. But we do know that he visited Richmond more than once to perform with his players before Queen Elizabeth at the Palace. Local legend says that he stayed with his friend Simon Bardolph at a house "at the end of a lane between George Street and The Green". So perhaps the house can claim some connection.

As we continue our walk around the Green, the houses on the left will strike us with their attractive 18th century architecture. No 3, Gothic House, may remind us of the mock-Gothic architecture of Walpole's house at Strawberry Hill. No 5 records the John Darbourne Partnership: we shall come across Mr Darbourne's former private house in our Kew walk. The building next to it, no 6, is modern infill, but has gained an award for the sensitive way it blends with the older buildings. One might argue that any building in a site like this should simply be a pastiche of what was there earlier; those with a more liberal viewpoint will probably be grateful not to be confronted by a tall concrete box filling the gap! Continuing along the Green, one may remark the fine bowl of stone fruits beside no 7, the intricate wooden carving decorating the doorcases of nos 11 and 12, and the delicate wrought ironwork and magnificent wisteria decorating no 14.

No 17 is remarkable on two counts. It was originally the very first coffee house in Richmond, established in the 18th century, when coffee was a rare and expensive luxury. Nowadays, it serves as a storeroom and a cunningly disguised back entrance to Boots. But also, early this century, it was inhabited by the writer Virginia Woolf and her husband Leonard. They rented rooms here from October 1914 to March 1915 because, with Virginia's precarious mental health, Richmond was felt less stressful than central London. In 1915 they moved to Hogarth House in Paradise Road, also in Richmond: it was there that they established the Hogarth Press (named after the house), and remained there until 1924.

Passing the Cricketers pub on our left, Paved Court straight in front of us has a delightful collection of old shops. At the end of it is the building of the Richmond and Twickenham Times, owned by the Dimbleby family for at least three generations. Richard Dimbleby was distinguished as a BBC commentator, particularly on royal occasions, and two of his sons, David and Jonathan, are following in his footsteps and probably equally well-known in their own right. Close to the Times building is the Open Bookshop, with a selection of books on the area.

Turning right, we find ourselves at the corner of the Green, next to Old Palace Terrace, completed during the reign of Queen Anne (1702-14). This would look splendid, were it not for a real eyesore in the centre: just two windows which were lengthened in the days before planning permission was needed for such a change. (One hopes that when this house next changes ownership, the new owners will be obliged to restore the original shape of the windows.)

At the far end of this terrace we see three particularly fine houses. Oak House dates from the 18th century, and was designed by Sir Robert Taylor, who also designed Asgill House, which we shall see later. Old Palace Place is slightly earlier. For many years, this was the residence of the late Sir Kenneth Clark, the art historian, former Director of the National Gallery, and onetime presenter of the TV series "Civilisation". He converted it into two houses, and lived in the right hand half.

Next to Old Palace Place is Old Friars, which was completed in 1687, as is shown by a date (no longer visible) on its lead waterpipe. It stands on the foundations of a monastery, from which Friars Lane also gets its name. Beaver Lodge next to this house was built in about 1720, originally as Assembly Rooms and a concert hall. Its elegant Georgian windows can be seen across the courtyard, looking through, or above, the gateway. Nowadays, it is used as a film studio, where Sir Richard Attenborough can sometimes be seen. (He is another Richmond resident, as is his brother Sir David.) The three houses across Friars Lane, while not strictly Tudor, do probably date from the 17th century.

A short distance further along the Green we see the magnificent facade of Maids of Honour Row. These four houses were built in 1723 on the orders of the Prince of Wales: the future George II. They were to accommodate the Maids of George's wife, Caroline, then Princess of Wales. Later on, in about 1830-40, no 2 was the boyhood home of the Victorian explorer, Sir Richard Burton. The splendid forecourts, railings and ornamental gates, may well have inspired a passage in Dickens's 'Great Expectations'. He describes Pip taking Estella on a trip: "We came to Richmond all too soon, and our destination there was a house by the Green: a staid old house, where hoops and powder and patches, embroidered coats, rolled stockings, ruffles and swords, had had their court days many a time."

Intriguingly, Dickens continues, "Some ancient trees before the house were still cut into fashions as formal and unnatural as the hoops and wigs and stiff skirts; but their own allotted places in the great procession of the dead were not far off, and they would soon drop into them and go the silent way of the rest." This seems to imply that Dickens had seen such trees, but they had gone by the time he was writing. There certainly seem to be no traces of them now.

Opposite the Maids of Honour one may notice the splendid line of iron bollards, decorated with a crown and the initials WR IV: King William the Fourth, who preceded Queen Victoria. These originally ran all the way around the Green; unfortunately, all except this section were removed for scrap metal during the war. The same policy resulted in the front railings being removed from almost all Victorian suburban housing: something more recently described as the biggest act of communal vandalism this century. As an early attempt at "recycling" it was perhaps laudable: and people did feel they were helping the war effort. But it is now generally agreed that the metal in most of these railings was unsuitable for use in munitions, and the railings were simply dumped in the North Sea. Perhaps one day the fine railings here will be restored all round the Green.

The Maids of Honour have left their mark in another way too. The "Maids of Honour tarts", a form of sweet cheese cake, originated in Richmond: indeed, there is little reason to doubt the old story: that an ancient royal recipe was purloined by one of these Maids and given to their cooks so they, too, could enjoy this delicacy!

Beyond Maids of Honour Row, the building behind the wall on our left is now called the Old Palace, and is the last substantial relic of the mighty Palace of the Tudors. Four centuries ago, the Palace was almost as large as Hampton Court. You can see how it looked from the Green, in a drawing made in 1562, reproduced on page 11. There is also a large model of it in the Museum of Richmond.

The surviving buildings of the Old Palace, beside the gateway.

The royal connections of Richmond go right back to the 12th century, but the Palace reached its final form under Henry VII. He named it "Richmond" after the earldom he held in Yorkshire, and he died in the Palace in 1509. When his son Henry VIII succeeded him, he used this Palace and the other at Greenwich as his main places of residence. But soon Henry was casting envious eyes on the even greater palace at Hampton Court, which his Cardinal Wolsey had completed in 1624. Wolsey decided to hand this over to Henry, telling him that he'd "always intended to give it to him anyway." (He would say that, wouldn't he?) For a time Henry allowed him to live at Richmond Palace in compensation, but Wolsey finally found it politic to live in a small house in Richmond's Old Deer Park. Henry meanwhile made Hampton Court his main residence. His daughter, Elizabeth, who became Queen in 1556, was the daughter of Ann Boleyn, and spent much of her youth at Richmond, where she was well treated by the King's ex-wife Ann of Cleves. The latter was lucky enough to be divorced rather than executed, and given the Palace as part of the divorce settlement.

Queen Elizabeth made much use of Richmond Palace, and it was here that she and her advisers plotted the downfall of the Spanish Armada. You should now proceed around the wall which encloses the Old Palace, and you find yourself at the original medieval Palace gate. And it was here at this old gateway that history was made at the very end of Elizabeth's reign.

Before her death in March 1603, it was still very uncertain who would succeed her to the throne. James VI of Scotland, as the son of the Catholic Mary Queen of Scots, was not likely to be a popular choice in England. So when the Queen died, in a room close to this gateway, her ring was taken from her hand and given to Lady Scrope, sister of a courtier called Sir Robert Carey. He describes in his Memoirs how he was waiting on horseback below the gateway, and his sister dropped the ring to him from a window above the gate. He rode straight to Scotland to convey the news to James, and the sight of the ring confirmed to James that his news was reliable. He immediately started his march to London, and in time was duly crowned as James I of England. Incidentally, Sir Robert's wife, Lady Carey, was later chosen as nanny for James's son, the future Charles I. Now if only she had written memoirs! Above the archway can be seen the coat of arms of Henry VII, depicting a griffin and a dog, either side of the shield. The small low arch to the right would have been for pedestrians, while vehicles went through the main archway.

After we have walked through the archway, we see on the left a long building with the remains of rounded archways in the brickwork, and Elizabethan chimneys above. It also has the distinctive diamond pattern created in lines of black brick: a reliable sign of Tudor date. It is still called the Long Wardrobe, having been used in Tudor times as a general storage building for items such as furniture or hangings. Now converted into three houses, we may notice a plaque recording one of them as the former home of George Cave, who was Lord High Chancellor of England, and Chancellor of Oxford University, in the 1920s. In front of his house is a fine iron gateway, with the lamp surmounted by a crown: a reminder that all this is Crown property.

10

Above: the surviving medieval gateway. Below: the Palace buildings as they appeared in 1561. The old gateway appears in the centre at the front. To the left inside the courtyard is the Long Wardrobe; across the courtyard is a more elaborate medieval gate, similar to that surviving at Hampton Court. (The two trumpeters on top of it can just be made out.)

Such are remains of the once mighty Palace. If we turn our view from the Wardrobe to look right, we now see the grand facade of Trumpeters' House. This stands on the site of the Middle Gate of the Tudor Palace, a small part of which is preserved inside, and which looked very similar to the present Main Gate of Hampton Court Palace. Trumpeters' House was completed in 1700, and takes its name from the statues of two trumpeters, probably heralds, carved wearing early Tudor dress. These originally stood on either side on top of the Middle Gate, and then outside the House which replaced it. They have now been moved inside for safe-keeping. Trumpeters' House was built for a prominent courtier, and among its later residents were Metternich and Marconi. Indeed, when Disraeli visited Metternich he described it as "the most charming house in the world". It was requisitioned by the government during the last War, and was then sensitively converted by the architect Bernard Brown, into six flats, leased by the Crown.

The modern housing which stands in Old Palace Court replaces some old cottages and stables destroyed during the War, but the posts and chains now here are probably 18th century, and formerly lined Old Palace Lane, into which we will shortly emerge. Passing Trumpeter's Lodge on our left, we enter the brick-lined alleyway which is guarded by bollards, this time of Queen Elizabeth II. On the right of the alley, however, is the distinctive small dark red brickwork of a wall from the Tudor Palace.

Old Palace Lane. The best preserved section of medieval Palace wall can just be seen in the distance.

Emerging then into what is Old Palace Lane, we turn left, and the attractive terrace of small houses we now pass on our right dates from about 1810. Adjoining them is the White Swan pub, and then a road lined by high brick walls. Almost at the end of it, on our left, is an ivy-clad wall with a square stone plaque summarising the history of the Palace. The plaque says Henry I was the first builder of the Royal Palace, though it was really Edward I who could be said to have turned it into a palace, from a simpler royal manor-house.

The first regular royal resident was probably Queen Isabella of France, wife of Edward II. He was the homosexual king who, as Marlowe's play describes, so alienated his friends through his blatant promotion of his favourite boyfriend, that Isabella plotted his death in 1327 and married his enemy Mortimer. The Palace was completely destroyed by fire in 1499, so it was Henry VII who was responsible for the building of the Tudor Palace we have seen.

13

At the end of Old Palace Lane we find the river in front of us. Behind the brick wall with the plaque lies Asgill House, which we shall come to in a moment. But looking to the right, we see no less than three bridges. The nearest is the bridge built in 1848. The railway line which runs along it used to be known as the "laundry Line", because in its early days the trains from Windsor did literally carry Queen Victoria's laundry to the laundry factories in Starch Green at Acton. Beyond this bridge is Twickenham Bridge, built in the 1930s to carry cars along the A316 west through Twickenham or east through Sheen. Beyond these is perhaps the most interesting of the three: the bridge above Richmond Lock, completed in 1894. As a detour from our walk, the lock bridge can be approached in a walk downstream along the riverside path. This detour is described in detail at the end of this first Walk.

We now look behind us to see the splendid frontage of Asgill House. This was built for Sir Charles Asgill, Lord Mayor of London in 1758. Though its shape indicates it might have been built on the foundations of one of the old palace towers, there seems only to have been a brewhouse on this site in Tudor times.

Not many years after it was built, the American War of Independence was to involve Asgill House. Young Captain Charles Asgill, son of Sir Charles, was about to be executed in retaliation for the proposed execution of an American soldier held by the British. It was only the intervention of the French King Louis XVI and Queen Marie Antoinette which resulted in the saving of both lives. So in 1782 there was a happy outcome in the return of young Captain Charles. Not such a happy outcome for the French King and his wife, who were guillotined just a decade later during the French Revolution.

Left: Asgill house. Right: the dovecot in the garden.

Just beside Asgill House is a magnificent copper-beech tree, planted in 1813 by the then occupant, a Mrs Palmer, to commemorate the birth of her grandson. As we start to walk upstream towards Richmond Bridge, we can see, over the wall, the top of an unusual white building which looks like a greenhouse. It is actually a dovecot, erected in the 1980s, on which white doves can often be seen perching. Further on, set on top of the wall, is a summerhouse with green-shuttered windows. Both buildings belong to the large garden of Trumpeter's House. Its main lawn now comes into view, with the river frontage of the House visible across it.

Shortly after this, we can look through the black railings of a garden gate, to see a fountain. This stands in the grounds of blocks of flats called Queensberry House. In the eighteenth century, beside the riverbank at this point, stood a large house occupied by the 4th Duke of Queensberry. This Duke used to sit on the balcony of his house admiring lady passers-by, while a manservant stood down below with a horse already saddled, ready to set off in pursuit of any lady who took the Duke's fancy. Unfortunately, the Duke was less appreciative of the charms of Richmond proper.

When a dinner-guest was admiring his magnificent view of the river, the Duke replied, "Why does everyone make such a fuss about the Thames? I'm fed up with it: there it goes, flow, flow, flow, always the same!"

After passing a group of early houses on our left, the last of which, no 1 Cholmondeley Walk, has had several distinguished artists as residents, we come to Friars Lane, which marks the boundary between the old Palace lands and those of the Friary. Next to the Lane we see St. Helena House and Terrace, which presumably took their name from Napoleon's place of exile, and were completed in about 1830. The terrace is carefully built above a line of boathouses which at one time showed the names of the families which owned them.

After the Terrace comes the White Cross Hotel, an eighteenth century inn which probably stands on the site of the Friary chapel. Nowadays, a different form of divine service is observed here, though both forms involve the use of alcohol. Next to the inn is the oldest thoroughfare in Richmond: Water Lane, with its ramp leading down to the River. Along here lived the watermen, who used to take goods off the boats and cart them into Richmond. The grooves worn by the metal rims of their cartwheels can still be seen in the cobbles higher up the lane. (Modern car tyres do not wear grooves like this.) Just across the lane, the building now a restaurant was originally a pumphouse, and appears in Turner's 1831 watercolour of Richmond Bridge, now in the British Museum.

We now come to Richmond's showpiece: the Riverside Complex opened by the Queen in October 1988. It was designed by Quinlan Terry and built by Haslemere Estates. Though there are always critics of any new development, most people are delighted that this part of Richmond has been restored to classical elegance. As the architect put it, "The lesson we have to learn is that if we want to put up buildings which are going to last for our grandchildren, we will have to build as our forefathers did." The complex is now mainly modern air-conditioned offices, though restaurants and an underground car park are also included.

Looking at the site from the river, one may detect that the site contained in essence four old buildings. On the far left was the old Castle Hotel. To the right of this, with a turret on its left corner, was the former Town Hall, a splendid Gothic-Style building opened in 1893. To the right of that, the red-brick building with the balustrade along the top is Heron House, which for a short time housed Lady Hamilton and Horatia (her daughter by Lord Nelson). And immediately beside the bridge stood the old Tower Hotel. In 1965 the Town Hall became empty, as the seat of local government had moved to Twickenham. (The new Borough of Richmond now incorporates Twickenham, and is thus the only London borough to embrace both sides of the Thames.) To the right of the old Town Hall, Heron House needed major repairs if it were to be preserved. So the Council in the 1960s planned to demolish everything, and replace the lot with concrete matchboxes. Thank goodness Richmond's amenity groups were active even then, and the public outcry raised was enough to block all such proposals for nearly twenty years.

By the 1980s historic buildings were better appreciated, and the result has been to incorporate the three major buildings in the new development. The old hotel with its ball-room on the far left was replaced by offices and a restaurant. But the architecture of Henry's, down by the river, followed an 18th century design for a royal palace which was never built. In the middle, the attractive Old Town Hall was kept and renovated. Heron House and Tower House were renovated and preserved, and now provide modern functions in their old buildings. In fact, the three black 'spiders' on top of the building next to Heron House, looking rather like the old chimney-sweep's brush, are actually rain-protectors for the central heating ducts underneath. The complex as a whole is something of which the town can be really proud. Let us hope more towns will follow their example.

Above: the Riverside Complex now. Below: as it appeared in about 1900.

RICHMOND FROM THE BRIDGE.

19.

Richmond Riverside in early 1992.

Looking upstream again, we see Richmond Bridge in all its glory. On its completion in 1777, it was probably the finest of all the Thames bridges: 200 years have given no reason to change that assessment, and is now the oldest bridge on the Thames as well. Before it was built, a ferry crossed the river on the same site, and it was the ferry's owner who proposed building a bridge there. The locals, and the authorities, pointed out it would be far better built across the river from the end of Water Lane. There would thus be a straight and level route through Richmond's main street, George Street, along Water Lane and across the bridge, without any need for heavy loads first to climb the hill, turn right, and then have a steep downhill slope to the other side of the river.

Unfortunately one influential person objected to the straight route. The Duchess of Newcastle, widow of the Prime Minister, owned the meadows opposite, on the Twickenham side of the river. In fact, she lived well away from the projected route, and only lived there for half the year anyway. But in those days aristocracy still ruled the roost: and eventually everyone had to give way to one obstinate lady. So the bridge was built on the site of the ferry, and that is why the traffic using this bridge from Richmond still has to climb the hill, turn right, and then drive downhill to the other side!

The bridge was built entirely on private money by the selling of shares, and tolls were collected at two fine Georgian tollhouses on either side: these tollhouses do not survive, but exactly the same principle of tolls is being used for the financing of the new Dartford Toll Bridge opened in 1991. Strangely, Richmond Bridge had no official opening, nor did it after widening in 1939. The one grand and joyful ceremony held on it was in 1859, after the death of the last shareholder, when the tolls were finally abolished, and free passage allowed for all.

As you approach the Bridge, you may notice that the benches beside you have elaborate iron supports fashioned in the shape of serpents. On the right, you may notice Turk's Bridge Pier: i.e. the Bridge Pier belonging to Mr Turk. He is the head of a family which has been in charge of "swan-upping" for many generations. This ceremony, now more than 700 hundred years old, derives from the fact that all swans on the Thames between London and Henley belong one third to the Crown, and two thirds to the Dyers' and Vintners' Companies. Every year three swan-masters, representing the three owners, identify and mark the new year-old cygnets to show their ownership.

After climbing the steps beside the Bridge, we may note a fine ornate lamp standard, presumably of the same date as the Bridge. A short distance further up, we can turn left into the new Riverside Complex. Walking through the archway we emerge in an attractive quadrangle with a fountain in the centre. Continuing straight on through the archway opposite, we look up to the river side of the Old Town Hall, with its five carved stone pillars lining a second-floor balcony. Turning right round the corner of the building, we come to the entrance to the Old Town Hall. This now houses Richmond's Central Reference Library, Tourist Information Centre, Local History Collection and the Museum of Richmond. It also has a cafeteria with a view over the river, which doubles as an art gallery for temporary exhibitions.

To conclude the walk and return to the Station, there are various possibilities. All of them start by turning right out of the Hall entrance and emerging on to the main road. On the left corner here can be seen a vine planted in 1840 and still growing strong. Turning left, the direct route to the Station is by following the main road bending round to the right and along George Street, Richmond's main shopping street. Usually thick with traffic, this street can perhaps best be appreciated if visited during Richmond's Victorian Christmas Shopping day, normally held early in December.

To explore more of the picturesque alleyways of Richmond, you can follow a more winding route. From the same point on the main road, turn left, then first left down Water Lane, right, along the river past the White Cross, then right up Friars Lane, and so back to the Green. At this point, you could turn at right angles to Paved Court, and go straight up Golden Court, left and left again down Brewers Lane, and then right and right again up Duke Street. At the end of Duke Street, the Station is a short distance left along the main road. Alternatively, we can use this place beside the Old Town Hall as the starting point for our Second Historical Walk.

Richmond Lock Bridge in about 1905.

A DETOUR: RICHMOND LOCK AND THE KILMOREY TOMB

As an additional walk which links with the above, you can turn right on reaching the river bank at the end of Old Palace Lane, and then visit three unusual attractions. Continuing along the river bank, you arrive between the rail and road bridge. At this point you can sometimes see, on both sides of the river, a small brick tower with a green roof. (These are normally only visible in winter: foliage obscures them otherwise.) Each tower contains stairs leading down to a pedestrian tunnel which was built by the river authorities, and runs all the way under the river to the other side. What an interesting attraction this would make, if opened to the public occasionally!

The approach to the Lock Bridge in spring 1992. At the top can be seen
one of the two toll houses. Up till the last War, pedestrians used to
be charged one penny to cross. Children used to pay a half-penny: but
some used to wait till after midnight, to avoid paying anything!

Continuing along the river path, we finally reach the magnificent Lock Bridge, which celebrates its centenary in May 1994. By climbing its steps, we obtain a fascinating view of the Lock from above. Upstream is a splendid panorama of Richmond Hill: the prominent red building on the hill being the Star and Garter Home, which we shall pass on the second walk. Downstream lies the magnificent elaborate river frontage of what was Gordon House, now part of the West London Institute of Higher Education. Gordon House was built in about 1827, but in 1851 was bought as his residence by the 2nd Earl of Kilmorey, whose tomb we shall shortly see.

Continue over the lock bridge to the other side: if the pedestrian walkway over the lock is closed, retrace your steps and walk across Twickenham Bridge. Whichever bridge you take, turn right on the other side and walk along Ranelagh Gardens beside the river. Follow the main road round the bend into St. Margaret's Drive. On this bend is a tall house with a white wall. Though originally a boathouse, it was converted into a recording studio by the rock star Pete Townsend of The Who. St. Margaret's Drive winds along until it ends near the Ailsa Tavern in St. Margaret's Road.

You are now in St. Margaret's, Twickenham, in the Borough of Hounslow, and just down the road to your right lies what is probably Hounslow's most remarkable tourist attraction. Above the tall brick wall next to no 260 St. Margaret's Road, can be seen the top of an Egyptian-style mausoleum. (It used to be visible from the top of the 37 bus when it was shown briefly on a TV programme presented by Lucinda Lampton: but the no 37 is no longer a double-decker.) It was built by Lord Kilmorey as a mausoleum for himself. Its first occupant, however, was his mistress Priscilla Hoste. She died young in 1854, though a son had been born to them ten years earlier.

Even as a young man, the Earl was undoubtedly eccentric, but he set what is still an unbroken record, by rowing from Oxford to Westminster non-stop in 14 hours! He later had a tunnel built under Kilmorey Road to give uninterrupted access to the mausoleum from Gordon House.

In preparation for his own death, the Earl used to lie down in his coffin and have himself wheeled through the tunnel by his butler, while wearing a coat of rats' fur, which he only wore when practising his funeral. He was duly interred in this coat in 1880, at the age of 92. His coffin now lies next to that of his mistress in the tomb, with a Roman marble relief above them depicting the dying Priscilla lying on a settee, with the Earl kneeling at her side, and their son looking on grief-stricken. (Neither of his two wives received such lavish treatment: they were buried elsewhere.) The grounds around the tomb belong to Hounslow Council, but access to them is not available at present, and the tomb is sadly neglected. (More details about Lord Kilmorey and his tomb can be found in "Railshead, Isleworth", by Alan C.B. Urwin, pages 15-20 and 49-53. Published in Hounslow in 1974, it is out of print, but can be consulted in libraries.)

As a variation on the return, go back down St. Margaret's Drive, but turn right into St. Peter's Road. Along here can be seen a marvellously varied collection of grand early Victorian houses, each designed by a different architect. We end up beside Twickenham Bridge, and can cross this bridge on foot to rejoin the riverside path. If, on the return walk, we cross back over the Lock, we can vary the route after crossing, by taking a small bridge across the stream which runs beside the river path, and then walking back parallel to the path, through what is in fact the Old Deer Park. This takes us past two obelisks, which were sighting points for the old Royal Observatory. This can be seen in the distance in the middle of the Park, and was built for King George III in 1769. But the astronomical instruments were sold after his death: the building is now owned by the Meteorological Office and used for weather observations. The walk then takes us under Twickenham Bridge, and past one of the two round brick towers mentioned earlier. Continuing, we arrive at a gate in the wall, next to the end of Old Palace Lane, which was the starting-point for our detour.

The Kilmorey Mausoleum in 1990.

SECOND HISTORICAL WALK:

RICHMOND HILL

The Old Town Hall stands in Whittaker Avenue. From the corner of the Avenue, opposite the old vine, turn right and walk under the fine clock and up to the approach road for the Bridge. Taking great care of the traffic, cross this road to the pavement on the opposite side, beside the romantically-named Joe's Bar-Grill. Just to the right of Joe's stands a tall obelisk which dates from the completion of the Bridge. It records that the bridge was built between 1774 and 1777, and on one side, mileages are given to places across the river, on the other side to places back towards London. We now walk uphill again past Joe's to the crossroads, and use the pedestrian crossing which takes us to the corner of Ormond Road. This is named after the Duke of Ormond, who was a prominent supporter of the Jacobites, and had to flee the country when he was impeached in 1715. We walk down Ormond Road, and see the grand Ormond Terrace on our right. This was built between 1761 and 1778, and almost certainly occupied by supporters of the Duke. There is a fine carved doorcase on no 6, and an attractive decorative roundel above the door of no 7.

Slightly further on, to the left, are two houses called The Rosary and The Hollies. Originally they formed one house called "Ormond Place", as shown by the tablet set in the brickwork at the front. It was built in about 1700 by Nathaniel Rawlins, a London merchant, and its first occupant was the artist Thomas Hofland, who painted several pictures of Richmond. Continuing to the end of the road, one sees two distinctive Georgian shopfronts on nos 24 and 26, with unusual wooden weatherboarding up above, known as "Kentish cladding". No doubt these two started as shops at the time when the Duke of Ormond's supporters lived in the Terrace.

At this point we turn right up Patten Alley. There are many alleyways running through Richmond: this one dates from 1762, when the land for it was bought from the then tenant, Miss Patten. Like many such alleyways, it is paved with fine York stone, and still has its original gas lamps with their distinctive shape, though of course now converted to electricity. We emerge from Patten Alley into the main road. This is called The Vineyard, and commemorates the vineyards which once stood in this area. These were cultivated centuries ago by the Carthusian monks who lived in what is now the Old Deer Park, on the far side of Richmond. (The Monastery was dissolved by Henry VIII.) At the corner of the Alley, on our right, stands Clarence House, built in 1696 well back from the road. Its builder was the same Mr Rawlins who built Ormond Place, and the house was until recently occupied by the actor Brian Blessed.

Turning left, and walking a short distance, we see on our left Bishop Duppa's Almshouses. The Bishop was Chaplain to Charles I, and set up the almshouses in gratitude for escaping execution under Cromwell, and living to see the restoration of the monarchy. Indeed, the plaque on the outer gate says in Latin that it is dedicated to God and King Charles. The main buildings we see date from 1851, but the tall gateway between them is in the Jacobean style of the original buildings of 1661, which stood further up the hill. This gateway sports a bishop's mitre, and has a plaque in the centre also in Latin, recording the original foundation.

As we retrace our steps back to Patten Alley, we may notice on the left Newark House, with its fine Georgian doorway, dating from the 1750s. Opposite Patten Alley are Michel's Almshouses. Half-concealed by the cottages on the road, stands the impressive main range, which dates from 1811. It has an extension to the road which dates from 1858, as announced by the white tablet on the end. We now continue to the end of The Vineyard and emerge at the start of Richmond Hill.

Though there are plentiful shops on our left, going up hill, on the right one can see a whole line of Georgian shop frontages which have all been converted to private businesses. The original shops are likely to go back to the discovery of Richmond Wells. In the 17th century, a well

The Old Vicarage School In Richmond Hill.

was discovered on the slopes of Richmond Hill, and in 1696 the Richmond Wells were opened to exploit this discovery. Like other Wells at places like Bath or Tunbridge Wells, they soon attracted the fashionable aristocracy, whose plentiful money led to the establishment of many gambling parlours. But there was the usual tussle between the desire to keep a thriving trade and its profits for the town, and the disadvantage of attracting undesirable elements at the same time.

While the Wells flourished, any shops setting themselves up on the slopes of the hill would do very well, as they lined the route to a major tourist attraction. Hence the former shops we saw on the right. As we follow the route uphill, we pass an attractive early Victorian terrace on our left – nos 28 and following – with its fine iron balcony running along the first floor. We then reach the Old Vicarage School, on the corner with Ellerker Gardens. One of the pupils at this school in the 1950s was Hayley Mills the actress, whose family then lived further up the Hill.

Historically speaking, the building was constructed of red brick in the 18th century, but refaced and castellated in 1809 in the then-fashionable Gothic style. (One may compare it with the similar Gothic House at no 3 Richmond Green.) Its first occupants were the redoubtable Houblon sisters. They were the daughters of Sir John Houblon, who became the first governor of the Bank of England in 1696. In the 1750s the Houblon sisters financed the setting up of the Houblon Almshouses, now located on the Sheen Road in Richmond. But their charitable feelings only stretched so far. By 1763 the Houblons had finally got tired of the constant rowdiness and noise from Richmond Wells, which stood almost opposite their house. So they simply bought the Wells and closed them down. Its buildings were demolished not long after. Once this had happened, there would be far less trade for the shops lining the Hill, so at a later point those we saw on the right, closed down. Nowadays, the main shopping street is George Street, leading from the bottom of the hill along to the Station. As in many other places, the railway arrived at a point out of the centre of town, where there was room for the tracks and a station. But once it arrived in 1844, the focus of shopping moved closer to the Station, as most outside customers arrived by train.

Continue up the Hill, keeping to the right-hand pavement. Shortly afterwards, we come to red brick pillars, the gateway to the start of Richmond Terrace. However, growth of shrubbery now prevents any view down from the hill from this point, and by keeping to the pavement we do have a view of the grand houses overlooking the Terrace. Continue along the pavement until you see the junction with Friars Stile Road on the left. This really does commemorate a stile crossed by friars: those same friars who cultivated the vineyards nearby. They used to take a daily constitutional walk up through the Green and along what later became Patten Alley, up as far as the stile which stood here.

The view from the Terrace Gardens in about 1900.

On our right now are a gateway and steps which lead down onto the terrace. (The disabled may prefer to avoid these steps and continue until the brick wall on the right changes to iron bollards and railings, marking the start of the Terrace proper.) By taking the steps down on the right, we can obtain a moderate prospect from this point on the terrace.

On the next level below is a large fountain with a statue in the middle. This is a somewhat robust Aphrodite, sculpted by Allan Howes in 1952, and popularly known as "Bulbous Betty". Steps on the right can take you down to inspect her more closely: but do not get too close. She was strong stuff in the 1950s: indeed, in 1958 a local Councillor McDougal said, "The statue is an incentive to young men to get married." (Given the current unpopularity of marriage in our society, perhaps we need more such Bettys placed in prominent positions?) But the Councillor did not explain whether she was an enticement, or whether one sight of her was enough to drive a young man straight into the arms of a quite different woman.

Continue along the lower terrace, passing the quaint old park-keeper's shed (which may remind you of the old Victorian cabmen's shelters used by taxi drivers in central London), climb up the steps at the end, and we emerge onto the Terrace proper. Continue walking up to and past the explanatory boards, which are sadly little use now for those wishing to admire the view (see end of book). The best view is actually behind: just across the road can be seen Downe House, which was bought by the rock singer Mick Jagger in 1991.

Walk a little further along the Terrace to where a path comes up to meet it: the path which has its entrance flanked by white iron bollards with attractive pine-cone tops. By standing between these, a moderately broad view can be obtained, which gives some idea of the fine view captured by painters in the past. The large Gothic building visible on the side of the hill to the left is the Petersham Hotel, built in 1865. The meadows below us are Petersham Meadows, now preserved in perpetuity; the large white house beyond them is a private house. To the right of the Meadows, the dark red building partly visible (but partly concealed by trees) in the distance above and to the left of the bend in the river, is Ham House, a Jacobean house now owned by the National Trust. To the right, it may be possible to discern a strange large building with struts sticking up: one of the grandstands of Twickenham Rugby Ground. Behind this, the location of Heathrow Airport can be deduced by the path taken by jet aeroplanes taking off and landing.

Looking now to our left, we see a puzzling large stone base (dated 1928 on top) surrounded by a hedge: in fact, a statue, now stolen, originally stood on it. Behind us, at the back of the terrace, is a line of memorial seats. The seat which is in a line directly behind the statue base, is dedicated to the memory of Sir Huw Wheldon, former resident of Richmond Hill, and presenter of TV's arts programme Monitor in the 1960s.

Continuing to the end of the terrace and crossing Nightingale Lane, we come to the grand house called The Wick. Built in 1775, it was at one time the home of the actor Sir John Mills. While living there in the 1950s and 60s, his wife the novelist Mary Hayley Bell did most of her

The Wick on Richmond Hill.

writing in an old Romany caravan which they kept at the bottom of the garden. It was here their two daughters Juliet and Hayley Mills grew up, and Hayley went to the Old Vicarage School which we saw earlier.

Next to The Wick stands Wick House, completed three years earlier, and specially built as a weekend home for the famous portrait painter Sir Joshua Reynolds. He was the first President of the Royal Academy, and his statue now stands in the centre of the courtyard of Burlington House in Piccadilly, where the Royal Academy is now based. Reynolds' ownership of Wick House house is commemorated by a square plaque on the front. Among those he entertained here were Johnson and Boswell, Oliver Goldsmith, and the actor David Garrick. Indeed, the splendid view from the back encouraged him to put aside his usual portraits and make one oilpainting of the view of Petersham Meadows spread below him. The house was damaged during the last war, and was restored afterwards as a nurses' home for the Star and

Garter. To the left of this house is a path which can take one down through Petersham Woods to the Meadows below. Avoiding this and continuing along the pavement, we arrive at the building for which Wick House is now an annexe: the Star and Garter Home.

This grand building is now officially entitled The Royal Star and Garter Home for Disabled Sailors, Soldiers and Airmen. It was designed by Sir Edwin Cooper, and was opened in 1924 by King George V and Queen Mary. There were several buildings on the site before this one: the first being a small tavern built in 1738; this later became a grand hotel: so grand, that for twenty years, Dickens used to hold an annual dinner there to celebrate his wedding anniversary.

Take the pedestrian crossing on your left and walk to the centre of the crossroads. You are now beside a splendid fountain with an elaborate iron cage around. This dates from 1891, and the inscription on top records that it was erected by the Richmond branch of the Royal Society for the Prevention of Cruelty to Animals. The four animals standing on top are griffons. These mythical animals frequently appear in heraldry: their popularity being based on their combining the physical (and supposed moral) characteristics of an eagle and a lion: two majestic and imperial beasts. The fountain spouts below also seem to show griffon heads. The sad plaque near them records that "the playing of the fountains was resumed to commemorate the coronation of George VI in 1937." Nowadays, litter accumulates so quickly in such fountains it is understandable that flowers have had to replace water in the basins.

Opposite the Star and Garter is a high brick wall: looking over this from here, you can see Ancaster House. This was built in the same year as Wick House, 1772, and it too has an elegant frontage. Using the crossing to reach this wall, turn right and continue round to the Park Gates. On your left, this part of Ancaster House is now the official residence of the Commandant of the Star and Garter Home, while the rest is used as additional accommodation for nursing staff for the home.

The Royal Star and Garter Home.

The wall around Richmond Park was completed by Charles I in 1637, but the present Richmond Hill Gate dates from 1898. In front of the Gate to the right, is a fountain in dark red granite, built in 1901 as a memorial to HRH Princess Mary Adelaide, Duchess of Teck. She was married in St. Anne's Church at Kew in 1866, and was the mother of Princess May of Teck, later to become Queen Mary, wife of King George V. One cannot help feeling that this fountain, and indeed the whole area, would be greatly improved if cars were no longer allowed to park all round it!

If you were to walk through the Park gates and keep to the right hand path, through the gate and along the path which leads ultimately to Pembroke Lodge, it is a short walk to King Henry's Mount. This artificial hill has a splendid view over the Thames Valley, but also, in the opposite direction, carefully preserves a view of St. Paul's Cathedral in central London. (This detour takes about 20 minutes return, though Pembroke Lodge further on is a nice place to take refreshment.)

Let us now retrace our steps to the RSPCA fountain, and then take the crossing which brings us to the hedge on the corner. Behind this hedge stands the first of the two grand hotels at the top of Richmond Hill: the Richmond Gate Hotel. These four 18th century buildings now form a delightful ensemble of different styles. Proceeding past these through the car park and down the short ramp, one comes to the second grand hotel, the Richmond Hill Hotel. This too is primarily 18th century: to the right of the Restaurant and Ballroom is what was a Georgian house, built in 1726, with its central doorway, and steps and railings leading to what was the front door. The two houses on either side of this were built in the 1820s, and now form part of the Hotel.

Continue to the far end of this car park, and look for Doughty Cottage. Its frontage, with an unusual decorative stone plaque, is just visible from the car park, above the brick wall. It was in fact specially built in 1915 as a picture gallery to house the impressive art collection of Sir Francis Cook, who lived in Doughty House, the large house next to it. The last of his collection was sold in 1965, mainly to galleries in the United States. The name Doughty came from its first resident Henry Doughty, for whom the house was built in about 1770. It was one of his ancestors after whom Doughty Street in central London was named, and no 40 Doughty Street WC1 is now the Dickens House Museum.

Beyond Doughty House, we find a fine range of 18th century houses, nos 4-1 The Terrace. No 4 dates from the 1730s, but the finest is perhaps no 3, built in 1769. The story goes that Mrs Fitzherbert was living at no 3 when she first met the Prince of Wales, later George III. They married in 1785, and spent their honeymoon here. After The Terrace comes the Roebuck Tavern, which has been on this site since at least 1720, when it appears with its old hanging inn-sign, in a magnificent painting by Leonard Knyff, now on show in the Museum of Richmond, and reproduced on the front cover of "Richmond Past" by John Cloake (1991). The tavern still has a fine view from its front windows.

The Richmond Gate Hotel.

At this point, cross over the road back to the terrace. From here, if you have time to spare, you could walk back through the attractive Terrace Gardens. Refreshments are available here, and you can walk downhill through the Gardens to reach Petersham Road. Alternatively, walk halfway along the Terrace and then down the footpath fronted by the iron posts we saw earlier. As you descend, the view stretches before you, while to the left can be seen the Petersham Hotel. This Gothic building of 1865 was designed by John Giles, who also designed the Langham Hotel in Marylebone. (The Petersham has a sumptuous staircase which rises four storeys inside, as well as a dining room with a magnificent view; it can be reached by walking down Nightingale Lane, next to The Wick.)

At the bottom of the footpath you emerge on to Petersham Road, and can then choose how to return to the centre. Both routes take you past the Three Pigeons Tavern, with its attractive views out onto the river. You might cross the road and take the path down to the riverside. From here, if you turn right, there is an attractive walk beside the river which takes you all the way back to Richmond Bridge. (Turning left along the riverside will bring you to the river frontage of Ham House.)

The architecturally interesting, but more noisy alternative, is to turn right and follow the Petersham Road back to Richmond Bridge past a variety of early buildings. Coming to the Three Pigeons, on the opposite side of the road stand four tall houses, nos 142-136, named Lansdowne Place and clearly Georgian. Further along on the left comes no 63, presently Walpole's Restaurant, dating from about 1760, and nos 61-55, of about 1720. After the next gap comes Hobart Hall, of the 18th century with later additions. The Duke of Clarence, later to become King William IV, lived here for a short time in 1790 while his own house in The Vineyard was being renovated. Opposite Hobart Hall stands the entrance to the British Legion Poppy Factory. The present factory building was erected in 1970, and it still produces all the poppies worn on Remembrance Day. No 39 is Bellevue House, as one can faintly read painted on it. This house of the late 18th century has a medallion in its side pediment, showing a figure playing a lyre. Past this house, nos 37 and 35 have moulded heads surmounting the big arches: these heads look the spitting image of Mr Gladstone, the Prime Minister of whom Queen Victoria complained that he "always addressed her like a public meeting". From here it is a short walk back to the Bridge.

Once back beside Richmond Bridge, you could return to the Station, or follow one of the variations described at the end of the First Historical Walk.

3) KEW GREEN HISTORICAL WALK

There is more than one guide to Kew Gardens, and little point in our adding another. Kew Green, however, is well worth exploring in itself, as is the little-known Thames walk beside it. So for those days when one feels like something different - or reluctant to spend over £3 on visiting the Gardens, this tour may be of interest. It does, however, end near the main entrance of the Gardens, for those who wish to visit them afterwards. Parking round Kew Green is difficult, so we shall follow our Richmond example, and start our tour from the railway station of Kew Gardens, more than half a mile away from the main entrance to the Gardens.

Facilities: at the time of writing there is one functional "Superloo" (10p to use it) hidden halfway down a dark alleyway immediately beside Kew Bridge, between the Kleftiko restaurant and the Bridge. No other conveniences are available around Kew Green or at the Station, nor, as we shall see, is there anywhere to have tea beside the Green except on Sundays. On any other day, one can have tea or a snack in Station Parade, either before or after the walk described below. The tea place with a particular Kew Gardens theme is the Kew Greenhouse at the end of Station Parade.

Kew Gardens Station is a neat example of finely-detailed Victorian architecture: built in 1868 principally of the commonly-used yellow brick known as stock brick, which when cleaned brightens up the scene greatly. If coming from Richmond, you emerge from the platform into Station Parade, ready to start the walk.

If you emerge from the Gunnersbury direction, on the east side of the station, you will see the proud words "West Park Exchange" at the top of the frontage of the building which stands on the corner of West Park Road. This commemorates the time when all telephone numbers started with a geographical name followed by four figures only, and each name had its own exchange. Just beyond the old Exchange is Kew Library, with noticeboards containing information about What's On in the area.

From this side, you need to cross the railway either by turning left and using the modernised subway, or turning right and using the footbridge. Unfortunately, its sides are tall and, being blank, covered in graffiti. As it happens, until 1990 there were attractive murals on either side: one a view of sunflowers, the other a progression of views leading from smoky inner London to the open air and the gardens of Kew. These murals were obliterated overnight with whitewash by British Rail without consulting anybody. Perhaps they think the graffiti are an improvement?

We now find ourselves in Station Parade. Many of the smaller shops here appeared within a few years of the arrival of the Station in 1868, but the two main red terraces in front of us appear to date from about 1900. The pub, called The Flower and Firkin, is now part of a chain of "Firkin" pubs set up by David Bruce in the 1970s to produce and sell their own Real Ale. The pub had originally been the station buffet, but in 1988 became the "Pig and Parrot", when the attractive conservatory was also added. It was taken over by the Firkin chain in 1991.

On our right can be seen Kew Bookshop, which sells several books about the local area. Next door is Alba Fine Art, but above its doorway stands a ship's figurehead. This came from the HMS Britomart, a tea-clipper built in the 1840s. (The Cutty Sark, now preserved at Greenwich, is the only surviving example of such a tea-clipper.) The figurehead was installed here in 1960 above his then antique shop by Ian Sheridan (a descendant of the playwright), after the ship, built by his great-grandfather, was destroyed by fire in the 1930s. Behind these shops stand factory buildings which were used to produce aircraft during the First World War.

The two parallel terraces of the Parade can best be appreciated by walking down to the end and looking back towards the Station. On the top end of each terrace stand detailed mouldings sporting fine and unusual red enamel name-boards boasting Station Parade: these are undoubtedly originals! Also at this end, the Kew Greenhouse cafe places tables and chairs outside in the summer, and has two old-style street lamps to look down upon those taking tea.

As we continue on the walk, we may notice litterbins sponsored by different local businesses: all credit to them. Walking down Lichfield Road, in front of us we can see at the end a curious thick white line. This turns out to be a piece of white concrete, sticking out from new entrance buildings to the Royal Botanic Gardens. These were completed in 1991, and the piece of concrete jutting out now completely spoils the view one used to get down Lichfield Road through the Victoria Gate into the Gardens. This new sculpture, if one can call it that, is in the best traditions of 60s brutalism: how was it approved in Kew in 1991? The answer, it seems, is that the Royal Gardens are Crown Property, and so do not need planning permission from anyone other than Her Majesty. Perhaps some day a more aesthetic sense will prevail and the concrete will be removed to restore the view. This would then enable us again to appreciate the magnificent stone vases crowning the gate, without having to go right up the them. The crown and initials of Victoria Regina (Queen Victoria) appear in the centre of the gate.

Turning right at the end of Lichfield Road, to walk up Kew Road, we may notice the magnificent water tower and chimney in the Gardens over the wall: it was built by Decimus Burton in 1844-6 to supply heating to the Palm House in the centre, which he also designed. As we come up to Broomfield Road, Lawman Court on the corner replaces 2 2 Kew Road, a sanatorium in which Felix Pissarro died from tuberculosis in 1897, at the age of only 23. He was the third son of the Impressionist Camille Pissarro, whom we shall encounter again shortly.

Crossing over Broomfield Road we come to the corner of Kew Gardens Road, opposite the Cumberland Gate, and then to Newens Bakery. This bakery prides itself on producing the local Maids of Honour tartlets to the original secret recipe. The shop was originally established in Richmond in the 18th century; bought by Alfred Newens in the 1870s, he moved it to this address in 1880. The premises had to be rebuilt after war damage, but the Newens family continue to run it today. It has a fine reputation, but is so popular nowadays it is virtually impossible to take tea there without booking.

As we shall shortly pass a group of cottages from the eighteenth century, that will serve to remind us of the real reason for Kew's prominence: the presence of a second Royal Palace. Kew Palace, which is now inside the grounds of Kew Gardens, was originally called the Dutch House from its architecture, when it was built as a private residence in 1631. Its first connection with royalty was when Queen Caroline, wife of George II, rented it as the royal nursery in 1728, and among those brought up there was the future George III. Even before that, the royal associations with Richmond, and royal ownership of most land at Kew, ensured a steady accumulation of courtiers living in the area.

Leaving Newens we continue to approach Kew Green, and on the way pass no 294, with its two bowed front extensions, a group of smaller cottages of the early nineteenth century, including a terrace built in 1831: nos 320 and 322 are particularly attractive, as well as the 18th century Adam House, no 352. Crossing straight over at the lights, and leaving the shops on our right, we start to walk up the right-hand side of the Green, and just past the shops come to the grand Bank House.

The name simply commemorates its more recent use, but its splendid balustrade and attractive doorways attest to its previous use: this building once served as lodgings for the Palace Guard of George III.

Passing the Coach and Horses, which was rebuilt in the last century, we look up to see a blue plaque on the corner of Gloucester Road. It records that Camille Pissarro, the French Impressionist painter, stayed here in 1892 with two of his sons. They were living in the first-floor flat above what was then a bakery. Camille came over from France in May 1892 because his eldest son Lucien, wanted to marry a Jewish girl, Esther Bensusan, but her father would not consent. Camille was no more successful in obtaining his consent, but in August the couple married in Richmond and Camille returned to France the same month. While here, Camille painted eight oils, and several watercolours, of Kew Gardens. But he also painted three oils of Kew Green from the front balcony above the shop. One painting was of the Church, while the painting looking north across the Green is now in the Musee d'Orsay in Paris. The building containing Pissarro's Wine Bar appears in the third painting. (For further details of the paintings, see the author's "Pissarro in West London".)

The three shops nos 10 to 14 have been here as shops for at least a century, then beyond them comes a group of Georgian houses. No 20 is the largest, with its five bays and three storeys; it was the retirement home of Gordon Lang, who was Archbishop of Canterbury from 1928-1942. No 24, Haverfield House, was the home of John Haverfield, Superintendent of the Royal Gardens during the 1770s. His daughter was painted by Thomas Gainsborough, and this portrait is now in the Wallace Collection in London. Further on, we may notice the attractive terracotta mouldings on nos 28 to 38, and after them, we come to the pond beside Priory Road.

At the far end of the pond is a slope, down which horses could walk to drink, and the iron rims of the cartwheels, which became very hot in the summer, would be cooled in the water. At that time, the pond was the end of an inlet joined to the river: indeed, a road nearby is still called Old Dock Close. But we also know that the watermen who brought Henry VIII on his barge up from Whitehall or Greenwich Palace, were paid to stop at Kew. So it looks as though Henry used to disembark at this very spot, and then ride the remaining short distance to his palace at Richmond. Thus even this humble pond has royal connections.

Just across the road from the corner of the pond, is a passage apparently called "Heavy Vehicles Next Turning".

Nos 68 to 52 Kew Green, overlooking the Pond.

To the left of this passage are two fine 18th century houses, nos 70 and 68, with attractive balconies on their front. No 70 retains its original front door and fanlight (the fan-shaped semi-circular window above the door); no 68 retains the fanlight above what was the front door, but the door itself has been moved around to the side, where a more imposing and slightly later porch now makes a grander entrance. No 72, to the left, now called Dolphin Cottage, retains its original Georgian shopfront. It must be one of the smallest houses in Kew Green, and all the more charming for it.

Looking to the right, nos 66 to 60 form an attractive and varied complex. No 66 was actually demolished in the 1970s by a developer who had grander ideas. The local council compelled him to put it back just as it had been: nice to find there are some things developers cannot get away with! By contrast No 60 has all the grace of its neighbours of the 18th century - but turns out to be late 20th century, and does in fact replace a warehouse on the site: a great improvement. It was built by the architect John Darbourne, whose architectural office was at 5 Richmond Green. Nos 56-52 are an equally delightful early terrace.

Willow Cottages in spring 1992.

Turning left down Cambridge Cottages, one can look left at the side wall of no 52, to admire three attractive Georgian windows: until you realise they are all "trompe l'oeil" and are painted onto a blank wall to make it far more interesting! Turn left at the next corner, past Westerley Ware Works, and follow the meanders of the pathway. Westerley Ware is probably a corruption of "Westerly Weir": there were numerous small fishing weirs all along the upper Thames, so at Kew there were probably two: with a second, easterly weir nearby. Just beyond the (currently) bright blue door of no 58 on the left, look up the passageway to the left, at the quaint wooden-cladded back extension of no 68 Kew Green, the front of which we saw earlier. Then follow the signs for Willow Cottages and Thetis Terrace.

In the gabled front of no 2 Willow Cottages is a fine stone plaque naming them. Willows are often a sign of water nearby - the Thames in this case. Unfortunately the plaque does not also date them. Though the style of lettering and gable might indicate the 1850s, the first reference to them seems to be in 1872.

Thetis Terrace in spring 1992

Thetis Terrace beyond them has a plaque which gives 1883 as the date of building. One wishes that more terraces would follow this example, and include the date as well. Thetis was a Greek water goddess and mother of Achilles. According to the Greek myth, she dipped Achilles into a river to make him immortal, but held him by his heel. This turned out to be his one mortal point, through which Paris was able to kill him during the Trojan Wars. (Hence the phrase "Achilles Heel".) Latin and Greek was of course the staple diet of education during the last century, so the original architects would be well aware of such allusions.

Climbing the steps at the end, we emerge onto the river bank. For those who enjoy river prospects, one can turn to the right and follow the path parallel to the wall. As well as a variety of attractive houses on our right, there is a view of Strand-on-the-Green across the river to the left. It is best seen shortly before one reaches the fine ironwork of the 1860s bridge (which carries the railway from Gunnersbury to Kew Gardens Station). Halfway across one sees an island, called Oliver's Island. This gets its name from having supposedly had a tunnel linking it with the Bull

Inn on the far side, where Oliver Cromwell is supposed to have held court during the Civil Wars. No evidence for this, of course, but why should one spoil such a splendidly romantic tale? In the early years of our history, such islands must have been very important strategically in controlling river traffic, and possible hostile action. And it is known that in the 1790s this one had a wooden "castle" built on it: used as a toll-house by those who wanted to recoup their money from having improved navigation along this part of the river.

Turn back at this point, and continue upriver along the towpath towards Kew Bridge. Before reaching the bridge we come first to Kew Gardens Pier, which allows river passengers to reach the Gardens, and has been here since at least 1900. Before the first bridge there was a ferry, and before that, the river was fordable where it faces Brentford, a short distance upstream. It is conjectured that it was at this point that Julius Caesar crossed the Thames in 54 BC, at what he described as the lowest fordable point. Beyond the Pier, we see on the left a children's playground. This is actually part of War Memorial Gardens, which are reached from a pathway beside Kew Bridge.

The present Kew Bridge is the third on the site. The first was built in 1758, while the second replaced it within a decade of the completion of Richmond Bridge. It greatly resembled this, was equally attractive and frequently painted by artists. In 1899 there were hopes of keeping but widening this old bridge. Unfortunately, the piers would have needed strengthening, and in those less enlightened days it was decided to take the easier option and demolish and replace it by the present bridge, completed in 1903. Thirty years later, when Richmond Bridge was considered for replacement, it was wisely decided to preserve and widen it instead.

Just before walking under Kew Bridge, look to the right to see two striking buildings across the river.
Both turn out to be office buildings: the taller blue building to the left, Flyover House, adjoins what is now the M4.

After walking under Kew Bridge, we find on the other side Kew Marine Boat Repairs, and a more extensive view across the river. The modern complex by the water's edge is the Thamesside Centre, an office- complex occupied by about five large businesses. It is still dwarfed by the old water tower of Kew Bridge Stream Museum, of which we now have a closer view. Halfway across the river is a bank with trees which gets wider to the left: this is Brentford Ait. The words "ait" or "eyot", both pronounced "eight", mean specifically an island in the Thames. The word seems likely to be even older than the Roman invasion: not surprising, when one remembers the strategic importance of such islands.

Opposite Kew Marine Boat Repairs are three white bollards which lead into a roadway. (The road is unnamed, but has "Kew Park Estate" on its corner.) Turn left down the road and follow it to the gate at the end, beside which is a small building. Looking back at its side wall, we find that it used to be a Ladies Lavatory, which proudly boasted both Hot and Cold Water. All this is marked in white tiles produced, as they proudly record, by Doulton and Co. of Lambeth. We now emerge back onto Kew Green. Turning to the right, we can walk past a splendid row of 17th and 18th century houses; there has also been a Rose and Crown Inn here since the 1720s. In walking past, we are interrupted only when obliged to stroke the friendly local cats. No 71 has a fine wisteria, and No 69 has perhaps the richest and most varied front garden. Almost all the houses here have balconies or verandahs, and no 67, the White House, has particularly fine fanlights, verandah and just about the most elaborate iron framework for window boxes one will see anywhere. Ironic that at the time of writing, these were left empty!

In the early years of this century, most of the houses along here used their ground floors for tea-rooms, with their back gardens forming enticing surroundings for those taking tea outside on sunny summer days. To judge by the comments of those who emerge from the Gardens nowadays, such a facility would again be greatly appreciated. One can still obtain tea, on Sunday afternoons only, from the Kew Tea Rooms, 108 Kew Green, on the east side of the Bridge (not far from the pond). From Easter to September one can also obtain tea (Sundays only) at St. Anne's Church on the Green. Perhaps some enterprising benefactor will start to provide it during the week as well.

From here, there is a little-known but very attractive

Kew Bridge seen from the Kew towpath in 1907. The building of the river wall along here to prevent flooding, sadly also prevents boats being hired from here, as they still could be when this picture was taken.

way of reaching three tourist attractions just across the river. These are the Kew Bridge Steam Museum, the Musical Museum, and the Waterman's Arts Centre in Brentford. If you walk from Kew Green across Kew Bridge, keep to the left or west side of the Bridge, and take the steps which lead down from the bridge shortly before it ends. These take you down to within easy reach of the riverside. At this point, facing the river, you could take a footpath to the left, to walk to Strand-on-the-Green. If you turn right instead, you find yourself walking along a delightful quiet path beside the river, with several houseboats moored next to the riverbank. After about five minutes, the path ends, and turning right you emerge onto the busy main road. From this point, both Museums are on the other side of this main road: the Musical Museum a short walk to the left, and the Steam Museum a short walk to the right. For the Waterman's Arts Centre beside the river, you turn left, but stay on the same side of the road, taking a slightly longer walk to reach it.

At the end of the fine houses on the north side of the Green, we come to the junction with Ferry Lane: a lane which led originally to the ferry which preceded the first Kew Bridge. Opposite the Lane entrance are two paths which lead across the Green. That on the right is bordered by trees and railings: this marks the boundary of a tract of land which King George IV enclosed in order to incorporate it into Kew Gardens. But his more benevolent successor William IV returned the land to the locals, so it still forms part of the Green. We however take the left-hand path, which leads diagonally across the Green towards Kew Church. Looking to our right, we can see across the road a house with a large white portico which juts out over the pavement. (It was built of course to protect anyone arriving by coach during rain, so they could step straight into the dry.) This house was the residence of the Duke of Cambridge, who died in 1850 and was placed in a grand mausoleum inside the church. He was the seventh son of George III (who had nine sons and six daughters). The Duke's daughter Princess Mary married the Duke of Teck in 1866 in a grand wedding in this church. It was their daughter Princess May who got engaged in Kew Gardens to the future King George V, but of course, as the future Queen, she married him in Westminster Abbey. We shall find many of the servants of the Duke and Duchess of Cambridge buried in Kew churchyard.

St. Anne's Church at Kew was completed in 1714 on land given by Queen Anne, but with several additions at later periods. The belfry we see above the entrance (which is at the west end) is part of the original church of 1714, but the elaborate colonnaded entrance dates from 1837 and was paid for by King William IV. The large dome at the east end, nearest the road, was added in 1884. Inside the church is a gallery, added by King George III to accommodate the Royal Family and their attendants. If the Church is open, a Guide to it and its monuments can be obtained inside. Perhaps the most curious fact about the Church is the mysterious disappearance of all its early records: this is discussed later in the Appendix. Let us then move straight into the churchyard, which is open at all times of the year.

St Anne's Church, Kew, in about 1904.

The entrance to the churchyard stands to the right of the church entrance, and is reached through a wooden archway on which climbing roses grow. A churchyard can be interesting to visit for more than one reason. In this one, horticulturalists may note a wide variety of unusual plants. Either it was looked after by someone with a keen interest in gardening or, possibly, birds feeding in the Gardens have brought across seeds which have flourished here too. At the moment it is rumoured that there are plans to remove many of the more eroded tombstones and place others around the perimeter of the Church. If so, one trusts that nothing will be done until a detailed survey has been made not just of the monuments, but the plants that surround them as well. This churchyard is also unusual for the variety of distinguished people buried here: some with royal connections and others connected with the Gardens.

Soon after entering the churchyard, we find ourselves walking over a large flat tomb. It is that of Jeremiah Meyer R.A. (i.e a Member of the Royal Academy), one of two distinguished German artists buried here, the other being Zoffany. Meyer was appointed Painter in Miniatures and Enamels to George III, and created the design for his portrait head on one of his coins. Meyer died in 1789, the same year as the French Revolution. Next to his grave slab is a large tomb with railings around it. This is the tomb of Thomas Gainsborough, the distinguished 18th century portrait painter whose paintings are to be seen in several of the major London galleries. Gainsborough died in 1788 at the age of 61, and the tomb also contains his wife Margaret and artist son Dupont, who died aged 42. In 1865 it was restored by another member of the Royal Academy, E.W. Ward, to ensure that Gainsborough's name was not forgotten.

In 1816, before that restoration, someone visited Kew to see the grave, and eventually found a sexton's assistant who knew where it was. "Ah," said the devotee, "this is a hallowed spot. Here lies one of Britain's favoured sons, whose genius has assisted in exalting her among the nations of the world." "Perhaps so," came the reply, "but we know nothing about the people buried, except to keep up their monuments, if the family pays. Perhaps you, sir, belong to this family, and if so, I'll tell you how much is due"!

Gainsborough is said to have bought a cottage at Kew so as to be near his great friend John Kirby: certainly, he visited Kirby frequently at Kew, and in his will asked to be buried near his friend in Kew churchyard. So if you hunt amongst the undergrowth near Gainsborough's tomb, you may find the large flat slab recording Joshua Kirby FRS (Fellow of the Royal Society). The slab is headed with a rather fine coat of arms, which includes two cattle, it seems. Perhaps it was designed by Kirby, who was an artist and, among other things, drawing master to Queen Charlotte, wife of George III. Kirby died in 1774 at the age of 58, so for the last 14 years of his life, Gainsborough must often have visited this tomb of his great friend.

Proceed down the steps, across the path and up the other side: we are still walking along the southern side of the Church. Then follow the path up to where it starts to curve to the left. On the left now is a tomb with a vase on top. The worn inscription on the other side shows that it was to William Aiton, "late gardener to his Majesty at Kew". He was appointed gardener in 1759 by George II, and should probably be regarded as the first true Keeper of the Royal

Gardens. He kept his post under George III (who came to the throne in 1760) and died in 1793. So distinguished was he that both Zoffany (see below) and Sir Joseph Banks were pallbearers at his funeral.

Next, go back to the path, follow the curve round to the left (which will shortly take you along the east side of the church), but turn off it to the right, to examine the tall tomb in the outer (SE) corner of the churchyard. This is a fine tomb decorated with "swags", or decorative leafwork, with the broad vase on top similarly decorated with stone ribbons. The tomb was erected for Thomas Gardiner of Bedford Row, and is unusual for having identical inscriptions on opposite sides. Perhaps the owner knew that such inscriptions erode over time: one side has clearly eroded more than the other.

Five spaces along the path, on the right next to the road, is the tomb of Johan Zoffany, RA, who died in 1810 at the age of 87. He was another distinguished portrait painter, particularly known for a group painting of members of the Royal Academy. He lived in a house which now has a plaque on it, across the river at Strand-on-the-Green. His wife, 32 years younger than him, joined him in the tomb in 1832.

Three places further along on the right, next to Thomas Catling Reeve, is the tomb of the Hooker family. The first, Joseph Hooker RA, was born in Exeter, and died in 1845 at the age of 91. He was the father of Sir William Hooker, who was Director of the Royal Gardens at Kew, and died in 1865 at the age of 80. His son, Sir Joseph Dalton Hooker, succeeded him as Director in 1865 and stayed for twenty years, during which he seems to have collected every honour going: his tomb records him as "OM, GCSL, CB, FRS, MD, etc. etc."!

Almost in line with the Hooker tomb, but moving to the internal (NE) corner angle of the church, underneath its stained glass windows, can be found the tomb to the Haverfield family, whose house we observed beside Kew Green. This records that one Haverfield was Assistant Quartermaster General of the Forces, while another was Chaplain to HRH The Duke of Sussex, one of the younger sons of George III.

Go back to the path, then continue along it until you see on your left a tall square pillar with two steps on top. This is to Edward Scard, who was Household Surgeon to The

Duke of Cambridge. The attractive stone vase which once stood on top of it, now lies below.

Now follow the path right up to the (NE) corner of the churchyard, near the road. Here is a fine horizontal tomb in deep red stone. Being perfectly preserved from the 1860s, one can tell this must be made of granite, which scarcely weathers at all, compared with the eroded marble or stone one sees all round us. The inscription commemorates John Smith, Curator of the Royal Gardens at Kew for 22 years from 1864 to 1886, and his wife. Their two children died aged 24, and the other, just two months. Continuing along this (north) wall we find, two rows along, a tall cross recording members of the Stapylton family, including Bryan Stapylton, who died in 1901 at Lichtenburg, aged 30, during the Boer War. Next to this is John Smith's son Alexander "formerly Curator of the Museum, and lately of the Herbarium, Royal Botanic Gardens." He too died at a very early age. Incidentally, the Herbarium contains much more than just herbs: it is the world's largest collection of dried plants, of great importance for research.

Further along the wall, but facing in the opposite direction, can be found a stone to Elizabeth Church, who died at Kew aged 82, and who "for upwards of 50 years was a most faithful servant in only two families, by all the members of which she was highly respected and truly beloved." So virtue sometimes has its reward! And next to her is George Gordon, of the Rose and Crown at Kew: the tavern across the Green. Continue along to the final quarter of the churchyard and round to the side entrance. Near the path here it is worth looking for a fine carved headstone depicting a weeping willow draped over a small casket. It records the sad death of Alice Marianne Tripp, an infant daughter who died aged four months: a further example of the high incidence of infant mortality even among the well-off in the last century.

In this quarter of the churchyard are several other monuments set up for servants of the Duke or Duchess of Cambridge. Two more elaborate monuments from the Georgian period can also be seen: one to Robert Wetten of Style House, Kew Bridge, the other to Captain John Smith. Having inspected these, we find ourselves back at the front of the Church.

APPENDIX:

THE SECRETS OF ROYAL KEW

We have already seen some of the many connections of St. Anne's Church with royalty. Pinned up in the entrance porch at Kew is a fascinating document with the above title. It is anonymous, but as its information has been freely available to any visitor to the church, it may be of interest to others. It can be summarised as follows.

St Anne's possesses an old iron chest which once contained the parish registers. The chest was stolen in 1845, and when found again the entire previous registers were missing. They have never been found since. Why did this happen?

The story goes that George III, when Prince of Wales, had married a commoner, a Quaker lady called Hannah Lightfoot, and they had at least one child, before he later married a royal bride. He is said to have married Hannah at St Anne's Church at Kew in 1795. His brother, the Duke of Cumberland, is also said to have married a commoner at Kew. Divorce was virtually unknown at that time, and it is thought that George III's first wife was still living when he married his new bride, Princess Charlotte.

What is known for certain is that in 1844, after Victoria had already been Queen for seven years, a Mrs Lavinia Ryves asked for £15,000 from the executors of the Will of George III. She claimed she was the grand-daughter of the Duke of Cumberland, and that her mother had been given a similar sum during her lifetime. Eventually she went to court, and produced documentary evidence which supposedly proved that her grandfather was indeed the Duke of Cumberland. The same set of documents also supposedly revealed the details of George's first marriage.

The Lord Chief Justice replied to Mrs Ryves that she was clearly trying to prove that all the sovereigns since George III should not have reigned, and that she herself was rightful queen! This is a curious reply, since the documents could only have shown, at most, that Mrs Ryves was a descendant of the Duke of Cumberland, who had never been heir to the throne. But what was dangerous was the idea that George and Hannah Lightfoot had had children, because such children might indeed have a claim on the throne. Whatever the implications, all the documents Mrs Ryves produced were dismissed by the Lord Chief Justice as forgeries.

There was of course one simple way to disprove all these allegations: to go to Kew and inspect the Marriage Registers of St. Anne's. Had her claims been false, the registers would have disproved them. But instead of that, the records were destroyed. In his family history "The Taylors of Kew", Mr Arthur Lloyd-Taylor recounted a story handed down through his family. According to this, in February 1845 his ancestor Henry Taylor was persuaded by a member of the royal household to hire two local men to steal the chest containing the parish records, and deliver it to the Taylors' house on the Green. The registers of Births, Marriages and Deaths were then removed and destroyed.

The establishment was clearly worried at questions being asked about George's earlier life. The resident vicar of North Woolwich, the Rev. Mr Bull, thought, for whatever reason, that his wife was the grand-daughter of George and Hannah Lightfoot. In 1845, presumably prompted by the recent court case, he came to Kew to try to find out more. He was a few months too late to consult the registers, but his interest was not welcome: soon afterwards he was sent out to the Falkland Islands, to be their colonial chaplain, and was not allowed to return for 15 years!

With hindsight, one can see why such a fuss was made. It was not so much the possibility of a new pretender to the throne. After all, Mrs Ryves or even Mrs Bull would have had far less claim than a male descendant, and any Jacobite descendants would have a greater claim even than them. Rather, it was a reminder of the former waywardness of George and his brothers, at a time when most people could remember both of them as ruling monarchs. The majesty of monarchy might be brought into disrepute. One could argue that the present Royal Family is to be commended for their greater willingness to face reality. Nowadays, if a member of the Royal Family is no longer compatible with their spouse, society rightly sees no objection to their separation or even divorce, although such a course is less likely to be taken by reigning or future monarchs.

All the same, it would be fascinating to know if Mr and Mrs Bull had children, and whether they have descendants now: as interesting as the more recent speculation whether one aristocrat in this country is the illegitimate son of the Duke of Windsor. He in fact seems rather proud of the possibility (and who would not be?): but he would not get far if he tried to claim the throne! There is another question: what happened to the documents produced by Mrs Ryves? They must have been handed in to Court in 1845: were they reclaimed by Mrs Ryves later, or did the Court decide to confiscate them? If so, one suspects that questions asked in the right archives (the Public Record Office just down the road, perhaps?) would not result in their being quickly produced. More likely, they have met the same fate as the Registers of St. Anne's.

ACKNOWLEDGEMENTS

I am most grateful to the London Borough of Richmond-upon-Thames for the privilege of attending their 1988 course for potential Guides to Richmond. At the time, I suggested they should produce a guide-book for the walks we learned about. This book is an attempt to meet that need. As it happens, the old Richmond Council did produce an excellent walking guide back in 1930, and another was produced by the Chamber of Commerce in the 1970s, but there has been very little available since then. The routes of the Richmond tours are similar to those taken by Richmond guides (apart from the detour to Richmond Lock), but the Kew tour is totally different.

Despite my attending the guiding course, I should make it clear that Richmond Council is in no way responsible for the opinions here expressed: such as the plea for action on Richmond Hill. Despite the suggestions made for improvement, I still feel that nothing can detract from Richmond being one of the most interesting and historic towns to explore in the London area. The fact that it has more listed buildings than any other London borough (including Westminster) speaks for itself.

I am grateful to Helena Caletta of The Open Book, Richmond, and Caroline and David Blomfield, of Kew Bookshop, for their encouragement. I am also indebted to the Blomfields and to Valerie Treasure for useful criticism of the sections on Kew and Richmond respectively: any errors which remain will probably be due to my reluctance to accept their advice. I am also grateful to several friends for comments at the proof stage. Needless to say, I would be delighted to receive any corrections or suggestions for a revised edition: they can be sent to me c/o Lilburne Press.

Nicholas Reed

RICHMOND TERRACE: A Plea for Action

Old paintings and engravings show that at one time there was a magnificent view to enjoy from the Terrace at Richmond. However, so much shrubbery has now been allowed to grow that, on walking up the hill even in winter, one can see virtually nothing until one gets to the explanatory boards which describe the view. Even here, the celebrated view from Richmond Hill is now just a shadow of what it used to be. Not because new building has obscured it - conservationists have at least stopped that - but because of the unchecked growth of trees.

Now, one can understand that people are more conscious of the beauty of trees than before, and that the damage caused by the 1987 hurricane has made people more anxious to preserve them and plant new ones. But it comes to something when half the view of Richmond Hill, even in winter, is now obscured by trees. For that matter, who thought of putting a whole line of trees in front of the view from the Hill? - this is the one place in the whole of Richmond where trees should be banned! Likewise, more distant trees, mainly growing in the Terrace Gardens, obscure most of the rest of the skyline.

As it happens, the drawing on the explanatory boards has faded so much that most points originally indicated on the skyline, and even the river itself, are now illegible. But in any case, of the 29 points of interest described on the boards, 16 of these are now completely obscured. Only one historic building is still half-visible: Ham House. It would surely not be too drastic to fell this one tree in front of the boards, and to lop about ten feet off the top of some of the distant trees: most of the historic view would then be restored.

At the back of the Terrace is a long row of seats, with many recent additions. Unfortunately, the view from all the seats here is greatly diminished by a two-foot hedge neatly planted in front along the summit: presumably by the same body which planted the trees. Again, why is this hedge here at all? Now we are more conscious of the needs of the disabled or elderly, it is all the more important to ensure a clear view for those sitting here.

About the Author

Nicholas Reed, BA (Oxon), MA (Manc), M.Phil (St.A.) obtained his research degrees in classics and Roman archaeology. He now specialises in art history, particularly the Impressionists, placing artists in their local context, and is a lecturer for the National Association of Decorative and Fine Arts Societies.

He has always been interested in South London and its history: from 1986-88 he was founder-Chairman of the Friends of Shakespeare's Globe; and from 1989-92 he was founder-Chairman of the Friends of West Norwood Cemetery. He now lives in Nunhead, in South London.

Other books by Nicholas Reed,
and published by Lilburne Press:

"Pissarro in West London": 1990
"Sisley and the Thames": 1991
"Pissarro in Essex": 1992

Lilburne Press
26 Hichisson Road
Nunhead
London SE15 3AL

Tel: 071-732 7778